Contents

Introduction

Long ago, candles were a necessity of life, providing precious light after dark. Today, scented candles are often used to create a warm and relaxing atmosphere, and to flood a home with delightful fragrances to create different moods. Coloured candles are used in interior design as focal points and to pick up accent colours in a room. They still have their place in religion and celebrations, too, to signify purity, peace and remembrance, and to mark rites of passage.

All candles are made of solid wax with an embedded wick to hold the flame. They may be made from paraffin, tallow (animal fat), beeswax, soya, palm or other vegetable waxes. When the wick is ignited, it melts a little of the candle wax. This liquid wax is drawn up through the wick by capillary action and combines with oxygen to keep the flame burning. As the process continues, the wax is consumed and the candle becomes shorter.

With the aid of the detailed step-by-step information and sample recipes contained in this book, you'll soon get started in this fascinating and fun craft.

Techniques

EQUIPMENT

To make the recipes in this book you will not need any complicated equipment; most of the things that you need will probably be in your kitchen already. You will, however, need to purchase the ingredients to make your candles. These are easily obtained from online candlemaking suppliers or high street craft shops. Here are some of the ingredients and equipment you will need for candlemaking.

1

2

3

Apron – to protect your clothing from splashes of wax, fragrance or colour.

Baking tray – either for use with cookie cutter candles, or in which to place your mould in case of wax leakage.

Candle wax (1) – soya container wax, soya pillar wax, beeswax blocks or beeswax sheets (see page 5).

Colour (2) – candle dye to add to the melted wax (see page 13).

Cooking timer – you may wish to set your timer to alert you when your wax may be melted. With experience you will have more of an idea of how long wax takes to melt.

Decoration (3) – appliqué wax, transfers and bronzing powders (see page 21).

Dipping container (4) – a tall thin metal container made specially for making dipped candles.

Double boiler (5) – or a bowl, small saucepan or metal dish placed over, or in, a saucepan of simmering water. You could also use a clean tin can with the side pinched to make a pouring spout. Alternatively use a crock-pot, electric casserole, stew pot or a professional larger-sized wax melter.

Goggles – to protect your eyes from splashes of wax.

Fragrance or essential oils (6) – candle fragrance oil that is formulated specially for candles or essential (aromatherapy) oils (see page 14).

Hairdryer or heat gun – gently heating with a hairdryer or heat gun can briefly warm the wax and smooth away any unwanted scratches on the surface of a candle.

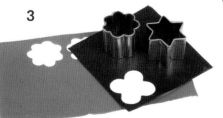

4

5

6

Kitchen foil or greaseproof/wax paper – you may wish to cover your surfaces to protect them from wax. You can also cover your cooker hob with kitchen foil to avoid wax spills, but remember that this may get hot. Soya wax can be cleaned up with hot soapy water.

Kitchen scales – if you are measuring your wax and fragrance by weight.

Knife – for cutting sheets of beeswax.

Ladle – metal or durable plastic for ladling wax into moulds if not using a pouring jug.

Measuring jug – made of metal, heat-resistant glass or durable plastic for measuring out liquid wax if using liquid measurements.

Metal jug (7) – with pouring lip, for melting wax directly on a cooker hob (and useful for melting small amounts of wax).

Mould (8) – metal, plastic, rubber, silicone, container, preserve jar, milk carton, any container that is heatproof and non-flammable. Cookie cutters for cut-out candles (see pages 6–7).

Mould seal (9) – a type of putty used to seal the hole around the wick on the base of moulds to prevent wax from seeping out. You could also use modelling clay or adhesive putty.

Oven gloves – handles can get hot when melting wax.

Scissors – for cutting wicks.

Spoon – made of plastic or wood. Plastic is best as it will not absorb as much fragrance as a wooden spoon.

Thermometer (10) – a wax, sugar or digital thermometer.

Warning labels – if you are selling candles or even just giving them away as a present you must always provide a warning label with safety instructions for burning candles (see page 25). Make your own labels or buy ready-made stickers to affix to your final candle.

Wax glue (11) – a sticky wax for placing on the bottom of tabbed wicks to fix them to the bottom of moulds to help keep them in place. A hot glue gun can be used in place of wax glue, or glue dots can also be purchased.

Wick (12) – there are various types of wick available to suit different types of candles (see pages 8–10).

Wicking needle – a large needle that enables you to wick your rubber or silicone moulds.

Wick supports/sustainers/bars (13) – small wooden sticks to hold your wicks in place. These include kebab skewers, barbecue sticks, chopsticks, pencils or cocktail sticks bound at each end with rubber bands, lollipop/popsicle or metal wick bars from candle suppliers.

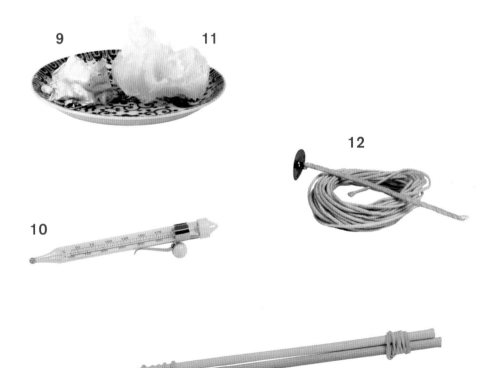

Types of wax

SOYA PILLAR BLEND WAX

This wax is a creamy white colour and comes in flake form. It is specially blended for candles that stand up on their own, i.e. pillar or moulded candles. Pillars, votives, wax tarts and aroma melts are all made with soya pillar wax. Two pours are often needed for this type of candle as the wax can shrink leaving voids on the top of the candle.

Soya wax melts at a low temperature and is therefore not suitable for tapers, dining candles or pillar candles of less than 2½in (6.5cm) as the candle will drip. Soya wax can easily be cleaned up with hot soapy water.

SOYA CONTAINER WAX

This wax is a creamy white colour and comes in flake form. It is specially blended for use in containers and cannot be used for freestanding candles. It has a low melting point and quickly becomes liquid when lit, creating a large 'burn pool' (area of melted wax). As the wax melts, the fragrance in the melted wax is released into the room.

Some brands of soya container wax offer several different blends of wax. Some are more resistant to frosting or 'bloom' (chalky white crystals) and are more suitable for coloured candles. Other blends have a better adhesion to containers and are best uncoloured. Read your supplier's information on each wax before making a decision.

BEESWAX

Beeswax is obtained from the cappings of the honeycomb and in its raw state has the most delicious honey-like smell. Beeswax is expensive and luxurious and can be used for all types of candle. However, it works particularly well for dipped candles and for latex rubber or silicone moulds.

Beeswax comes in the form of yellow pellets or blocks that retain all of the wonderful honey scent. Unfragranced, or deodorized bleached white beeswax pellets can be purchased if you wish to add scent and colour to your beeswax candle, or you can refine the wax from your own beehives.

Note Beeswax can also be used for making container candles, however I would recommend soya container wax as a first choice.

A beeswax block.

In tray from left to right: soya pillar blend, white beeswax pellets and soya container wax.

Moulds and containers

METAL PILLAR MOULDS

These are the best and most durable moulds to use, but they can be expensive. Metal moulds are usually seamless to give a good crisp finish to your candle. They are generally available in round, square, octagon and star shapes. Soya pillar blend wax or beeswax is used with these moulds. The moulds can last for many years and should be a good investment.

CONTAINERS

The advantage of making a container candle is that the container is also the mould and any liquid wax remains inside the container. This also helps to protect your carpets and furniture from wax spillage.

Soya container wax is poured directly into heat-resistant containers such as storage jars, plant pots, garden urns, apothecary jars, preserve jars, tea lights, metal tins, old tin cans, glass containers (as long as they are thick enough or heat proof), shells, silver pots and metal buckets. Make sure that your containers are clean and free from debris.

POLYCARBONATE OR PLASTIC MOULDS

These moulds come in interesting shapes such as hearts, eggs, rounds, pyramids and pentagons as well as round and square pillars. You can also buy polycarbonate or plastic moulds with several impressions on one sheet for making votives or floating candles. Long-term use of essential oils or fragrance may damage polycarbonate or plastic moulds. You may get a seam of wax if using a two-part mould but this can easily be removed with a knife.

OTHER MOULDS

Providing that your wax is not poured at too high a temperature, plastic, metal, rubber or cardboard items from around the house can be used as moulds. Look around your home for suitable items such as margarine tubs, yoghurt pots, plastic drawer tidies, cardboard boxes, empty popcorn buckets, potato chip/crisp tubes, food storage tubs, tin cans, empty sweet or candy tins, biscuit tins, milk or juice cartons.

LATEX RUBBER AND SILICONE MOULDS

These moulds are often used to create intricate designs, interesting textures or unusual shapes. A whole host of amazing rubber or silicone moulds are available from intricate flowers, fruits, beehives and animals, to dinner candles and interestingly shaped pillar moulds. Most beekeeping suppliers usually have a good range of these type of moulds. When using beeswax for moulded or pillar candles you will need to spray your mould first with silicone spray or vegetable oil for easy release.

These moulds will require a wicking needle so that you can make a hole in the rubber through which to thread the wick. Use beeswax with these moulds, or you can use soya pillar blend wax as long as the diameter of the soya candle is a minimum of 2½–3in (6.5–7.5cm) so that a ½in (1cm) wall is created in the first inch of burning to prevent wax leakage.

Preparing moulds

Soya wax should be self-releasing. If the soya wax does stick to your mould, or if you are using beeswax, you can use silicone spray or vegetable oil to coat your mould first for easy release. Always check your moulds for scratches as any marks will leave an impression on the candle.

Cleaning moulds

There is no need to wash your moulds unless they are particularly dirty or smelling strongly of fragrance. Wash them with warm soapy water.

MAKING LATEX RUBBER MOULDS

You can easily make your own moulds at home using latex liquid rubber. It is particularly good for getting into little crevices and for picking up intricate details and texture. Have a look around the home or in the natural world for interesting objects such as citrus fruits or pine cones.

1 You can either paint the liquid latex on to the object (stand it on an upturned mug or bowl), or dip it straight into the liquid latex.

2 If the crevices are particularly deep, dipping is recommended.

3 Leave each layer to set slightly before applying the next and keep building them up. This may take quite a few dips, but you can also use latex rubber gel, which is thicker than the liquid and will build up the thickness more quickly. However, the latex is surprisingly strong and you will often only need to create a thickness of a few millimetres.

4 Leave the mould to set overnight then gently peel away. Use your homemade mould in the same way as you would with any other rubber mould (see page 16).

Selecting a wick

WHAT IS A WICK?

A wick is a specially made combination of braided cotton plies, or wood, set within a candle. It consumes melted wax like fuel to keep the flame burning. To achieve the best burn, choosing the right wick is the most important part of candlemaking.

If the wick is too small it will not draw up enough melted wax and the candle can drip. If the wick is too big, the candle could burn too quickly causing smoke or mushrooming (see Troubleshooting on page 26). By choosing the correct wick, your candle should consume all of the wax at the right pace, with no dripping, and should produce a good steady flame approximately 1in (2.5cm) high.

Each type and size of candle, blend and brand of wax, fragrance, essential oil, colour and wick will react differently with each other. As each combination of these factors is unique, it is impossible to indicate the exact wick to use in your candle. Only by test burning (see page 23) will you find the best wick for your candle.

However, the wick guide opposite gives you suggested starting points for wick testing. These are recommendations only and are not limited to the wicks suggested. You should always fully test burn a candle to find the most suitable wick.

TYPES OF WICK

Only 'candle' wicks should be used in candles. Never use string, twine, rope or sticks. They may look similar, but wicks have been developed to burn safely. Modern wicks curl over slightly at the tip so that the carbon burns off and does not build up or mushroom. Using anything that is not a candle wick is a fire hazard. Always trim wicks to ¼in (0.5cm) before burning.

There are many types of wick available. However, not all are suitable for use in beeswax or soya wax candles. Below and opposite are some of the recommended wicks to use.

Flat-braided wicks – LX series

A self-trimming thin, flat wick that curls into the flame minimizing carbon build-up or mushrooming. This wick helps to centralize the heat, preventing overheating of containers and tunnelling in pillar candles. Use these wicks with soya wax.

ECO multipurpose wick series

A flat, coreless cotton wick with thin interwoven paper filaments/threads providing a controlled self-trimming effect, which reduces mushrooming, soot and smoke. Use these wicks with soya wax.

Tea light wicks – TL wick series

A tightly braided non-cored flat wick designed for tea lights and small candles. Self-trimming with a slight curl, minimizing carbon build-up or mushrooming. It provides a controlled flame with greater safety in metal and plastic tea light cups. Use these wicks with soya wax.

Wood wicks

These provide the soft crackling sound of a wood fire. The amount of crackle that you get from your candle may depend on the reaction between your fragrance and colour; the more you use, the more your candle may crackle. Trim the wick before burning and light the whole of the wick. These wicks are for use with natural waxes.

Square-braided wicks

Bleached cotton wicks for use with moulded, pillar and dipped beeswax candles. Designed to curl slightly as the candle burns to avoid carbon build-up and mushrooming. Use these wicks with beeswax.

Cored wicks

You may see wicks with metal, paper or cotton cores for sale. However, these are not recommended for use with soya candles.

A selection of wicks, from left to right: unwaxed wick, pre-waxed cut wicks, wooden wicks and pre-tabbed waxed wicks.

WICK GUIDE

These wick recommendations are suggestions only and you may wish to try other types or sizes of wick. If you have a pillar candle that is an uneven shape, take the average diameter from the middle of the candle to work out wick size.

Candle diameter (in)	Candle diameter (mm)	Wick suggestions for initial burn testing
Soya container candles		
Tea light (or tiny container)	Tea light (or tiny container)	TL10, TL13, TL15, TL18, TL21, TL25, TL28, TL31
1–2in	25–50mm	LX8, LX10, ECO0.5, ECO1, ECO2
2–2½in	50–65mm	LX12, LX14, ECO1, ECO2, ECO4, ECO5
2½–3in	65–75mm	LX14, LX16, LX18, ECO4, ECO5, ECO6, ECO8, ECO10
3–3½in	75–90mm	LX18, LX20, LX22, LX24, LX28, ECO10, ECO12, ECO14
3½–4in	90–100mm	LX26, LX28, LX30, ECO14, ECO16
4in plus	100mm plus	You will need to use two or more evenly spaced wicks
Soya pillar candles		
Votive	Votive	LX10, LX12, LX14, ECO1, ECO2, ECO4
2–2½in	50–65mm	LX12, LX14, ECO1, ECO2, ECO4, ECO5
2½–3in	65–75mm	LX14, LX16, LX18, ECO4, ECO5, ECO6, ECO8, ECO10
3–3½in	75–90mm	LX18, LX20, LX22, LX24, LX28, ECO10, ECO12, ECO14
3½–4in	90–100mm	LX26, LX28, LX30, ECO14, ECO16
4in plus	100mm plus	You will need to use two or more evenly spaced wicks
Beeswax candles – NT wicks		
Votive	Votive	NT29, NT32, NT35
Tea lights/small candles 1–2in	Tea lights/small candles 25–45mm	NT20, NT23, NT26
1½–21/8in	35–55mm	NT29, NT32, NT35
2–2½in	45–65mm	NT38, NT41, NT44, NT47
2½–3in	60–75mm	NT53, NT59
3–3½in	75–90mm	NT65, NT71
Beeswax candles – square-braided wicks		
¼in	6mm	No.0
½in	13mm	No.1
¾in	19mm	No.1A
1in	25mm	No.2
1¼in	32mm	No.3
1½in	38mm	No.4
1¾in	45mm	No.5
2in	50mm	No.6
2½in	65mm	No.7
4in	100mm	No.8
Wood wicks		
2in	50mm	Small
2¾–3⅛in	70–80mm	Medium
4in	100mm	Large

PURCHASING AND PREPARING YOUR WICK

Once you have selected your wick size and type, choose the length required – wick can be purchased by the roll or pre-cut. Measure the length of your mould and select a wick that is 1–2in (2.5–5cm) longer so that it can easily be tied or held in place with wick sustainers. It is better to select more wick than needed and cut off the excess when the candle is set, than to be short.

PRIMING A WICK

For all recipes you will need a primed wick. This is simply a wick that has been dipped and coated in wax. Priming a wick aids the initial lighting of your candle. It will also stiffen it, helping it to stand up in container candles and will make it easier to thread through holes in moulded candles. You can either prime your own wick, following the instructions below, or you can purchase them ready-primed.

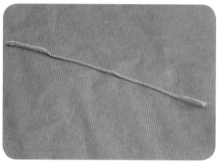

IMPORTANT
Make sure that you wick your candle appropriately for the type of candle you are making. See pages 15–22 to find out how to wick individual types of candles.

1 To prime your own wick first dip the wick in liquid wax to coat it.

2 Leave the wick lying straight on a piece of greaseproof or wax paper for a few minutes until set. The only exception to this rule is for dipped candles. By the very nature of the dipping process you are effectively priming your candle with the first dip.

TABBED WICKS

If you are making a container candle, consider using a 'tabbed wick' (a wick with a round metal tab fixed to one end). Apply glue to the base of the metal tab and secure it to the bottom of your container, this will help to keep the wick in place. You can purchase pre-tabbed waxed (primed) wicks in different lengths, or you can buy the tabs separately, affix to the bottom of your primed wick, and crimp the ends to secure.

Basic method

MEASURING AND WEIGHING WAX

METHOD ONE
Calculate the amount of liquid wax needed:
Fill the mould with water (block any holes with mould seal), pour the water into a measuring jug and measure the liquid; use the same amount of liquid wax.

METHOD TWO
Calculate the weight of unmelted wax needed:
Fill the mould with water (block any holes with mould seal). Pour the water into a measuring jug and measure the liquid. Water weighs approximately the same as its liquid measurement (i.e. 1 litre of water = 1kg of water); however, wax weighs 15 per cent less. Therefore, divide the liquid water measurement measure by 1.15. For example:
measurement of water = 150ml ÷ 1.15 = 4.5oz (130g) unmelted wax

METHOD THREE
Measure the proportional size of the container to the wax:
Using wax flakes or pellets, measure 1½ times the size of the container, i.e. for a one cup container use 1½ cups of wax.

It is always best to overestimate the amount of wax needed as it is difficult to quickly melt, fragrance and colour more wax if you are short while at a crucial stage of making. You may also need extra wax for a second pouring of pillar candles. Any leftover wax can always be kept and re-used.

CONVERSION TABLE OF WATER TO WEIGHT OF WAX

Water (ml) (or ml of liquid wax)	= Weight of unmelted wax (oz)	= Weight of unmelted wax (g)
50ml	= 1.5oz	= 43g
100ml	= 3oz	= 85g
150ml	= 4.5oz	= 130g
200ml	= 6oz	= 175g
300ml	= 9oz	= 260g
400ml	= 12oz	= 350g
500ml	= 15oz	= 425g
1 litre	= 30oz	= 850g

MELTING WAX

Set the cooking timer for 20 minutes so that you do not forget the melting wax. Use a double boiler (one pan sits half inside the other, which is filled with simmering water). This provides a gentle heat underneath. All beeswax should be heated this way. You could also use a heat-resistant glass or metal jug, or a bowl placed over a saucepan of water.

1 Turn on the heat source for the melting pot and gently melt the wax in the double boiler. Do not leave melting wax unattended at any time as wax can combust.

2 Make sure that the water in the double boiler does not boil dry. After 20 minutes check that the wax has melted.

ALTERNATIVE WAYS OF HEATING WAX

If you are extremely careful you can heat the soya wax (not beeswax) in a metal container directly on the cooker hob, but you must make sure that the wax is heated up very gently and doesn't overheat.

Another idea is to melt the wax in an electric casserole dish or stew pot/crock-pot. Professional pots and melters can also be purchased.

Metal container on cooker hob

Professional melter

WAX MELTING AND POURING

Use the following wax temperature table to heat the wax to the required temperature. Never heat your wax above 200°F (93°C). Not only can high temperatures be extremely dangerous, but also heating the wax too high can cause it to discolour and may affect the burn quality of the candle. The wax should melt fairly quickly, so always stay in the room during this process, and set your cooking timer as a reminder. Test the temperature with a cooking thermometer by dipping it into the wax and immediately wiping it off with kitchen roll. Alternatively, use a digital thermometer. If adding powdered dye, heat the wax to 190°F (87°C) so that the powder completely dissolves.

WAX MELTING TEMPERATURES

Type of wax	Melting temperature	Melting temperature if using powder dye	Pouring temperature
Container blend (containers and tea lights)	155°F (68°C)	190°F (87°C)	125°F (51°C) 155°F (63°C) (tall, thin jars)
Pillar blend (pillars, moulded, votives, tarts)	165°F (73°C)	190°F (87°C)	1st pour 155°F (63°C) 2nd pour 145°F (62°C)
Beeswax (pillars, moulded, votives)	165°F (73°C)	190°F (87°C)	155°F (68°C)

IMPORTANT

This table is a guide only and you should refer to your manufacturer's instructions, or supplier's details, for specific instructions on melting your wax as each brand of wax may require slightly different melting and pouring temperatures. You can pour as low as 100°F (37°C) as long as you keep stirring the wax.

ADDING THE COLOUR

Liquid, chip and block dyes can all be added to wax at 155°F (68°C) and at 190°F (87°C) for powder dyes. Pre-coloured beeswax blocks can also be purchased. Colour can fade in the light, but UV inhibitors can be purchased to add to the wax to help prevent colour loss.

1 Heat the wax to the required temperature and add the colour.

2 Stir thoroughly until it is completely dissolved. Candle colour tends to be fairly concentrated so only add a little to start with; you can always add more. Melted candle wax will always look much darker than the set wax, which will set much paler.

3 To get an idea of the colour that the candle will be when set, spoon a little coloured candle wax on to a piece of greaseproof paper or on to a plastic tray, leave for a few minutes until set, if the colour is too pale simply add more colour to the melting pot.

ADDING THE CANDLE FRAGRANCE OR ESSENTIAL OIL

It is very important that you only use a fragrance that is sold as a candle fragrance oil. For instance, a soap-making or potpourri fragrance may actually be dangerous to use in a candle. This is because the flash point (the point at which it catches fire) could be too high if the fragrance contains alcohol.

An 'apple pie' fragrance from one company could be made with different ingredients from a fragrance with the same name from another company. Remember to ask your supplier if any of their fragrances have been tested with the brand of wax that you are using.

If a fragrance is not compatible with your candle it can cause the wax to sweat, frost or bloom. It may create a small burn pool or poor scent throw, or it could also cause an inferior burn with mushroom or sooting, a lumpy surface or bad adhesion to the sides of a container candle. If your candle displays any of these symptoms it could be the type of fragrance that you are using and you may wish to try a similar fragrance from another supplier. However, it could also be the wrong choice of wick, or the pouring temperature that is causing one of these problems, so it may be a good idea to try another wick or pouring temperature before purchasing a different candle fragrance oil. You could also try re-making your candle using less of the candle fragrance oil.

Essential oils can also be used for their wonderful aromas and therapeutic scents, and again testing for suitability in your candle is important. Before buying large quantities of fragrance, always make sure that you have fully test-burned your candles (see page 23).

ADDING THE ESSENTIAL OIL OR FRAGRANCE

1 Add the fragrance or essential oil last to prevent evaporation and so the latter do not lose their therapeutic properties. Adding the fragrance may cool the wax slightly.

2 Make sure that you stir in your fragrance or essential oil thoroughly into the melted wax.

AMOUNT OF SCENT TO USE

The recommended amount of fragrance to use in candles is up to 10 per cent for candle fragrance oils and up to 5 per cent for essential oils. This means that for 5 per cent you should use 5ml (or 1 teaspoon) per 100ml of liquid wax.

If you are making candles professionally, it is best to work out the amounts of fragrance by weight as large amounts are sold in this way. This is because some

essential oils weigh more than others. Weigh the amount of liquid fragrance/essential oils. Five per cent of 100g (3½oz) = 5g (0.18oz), etc.

For all of the recipes in this book we have used approximately 5 per cent fragrance or essential oils. Essential oils can be expensive so you can always use less than the amount specified in the recipes to save on costs, or use a

fragrance oil instead (fragrance oils are cheaper than essential oils). Or, if you wish to have a more strongly scented candle you will need to increase the amount of candle fragrance oil (not essential oils) to a maximum of 10 per cent. Bear in mind that by increasing the fragrance levels you take the risk of possibly reducing the burn quality of your candle.

POURING THE WAX

When the coloured and fragranced wax is at the correct temperature, gently pour it into the mould. If you have a melting pot without a spout, you may find it easier to ladle the wax into the mould with a plastic or metal ladle.

If you are making container candles, the containers should be at room temperature. If they are very cold, gently heat them up in the oven or warm them with a hairdryer. Containers and moulds should be placed at least ½in (1.5cm) apart so that air can circulate freely between each candle.

Candles should not be cooled too quickly; the temperature of the room should be around 70°F (21°C). The candle should now be left undisturbed to set for at least 48 hours.

> **CAUTION**
> If you have excess wax, pour it into a yoghurt pot or plastic container for re-use. Never pour melted wax down the drain. It will solidify and cause a blockage.

Types of candlemaking

PILLAR AND MOULDED CANDLES

Both pillar and moulded candles are freestanding candles that are made in moulds (metal, polycarbonate, plastic, rubber or silicone, or sand) using either beeswax or a special soya pillar wax. As the first inch (2.5cm) of a pillar candle burns down, a wall of wax should form around the sides of the candle, which keeps the liquid wax contained.

As well as beeswax, soya pillar blend wax can be used to make pillar moulds as long as the diameter is a minimum of 2½–3in (6.5–7.5cm) to enble the wall to form during burning and prevent wax leakage. If you are using beeswax, spray your mould with silicone mould release, or coat it with vegetable oil to make unmoulding easier.

1 Take a primed wick (see page 10) and feed it through the holes in the mould.

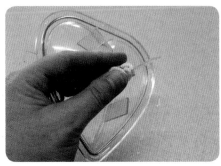

2 Seal with mould seal, modelling clay or adhesive putty to prevent any liquid wax from escaping.

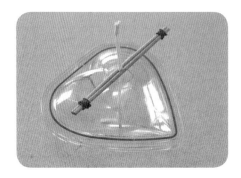

3 Place the other end of the wick between the two sticks of the wick sustainer and pull gently so that the wick is taut and centrally positioned in the mould (otherwise the candle will burn unevenly). If you do not have wick sustainers you could tie the end of a wick to a skewer or chopstick – you will need to cut a slightly longer piece of wick to allow for this.

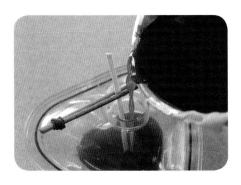

4 Melt, colour and fragrance the soya pillar wax or beeswax and pour at the correct temperature (see page 12), retaining some wax for the second pour. Leave the candle to set for a short while. You may notice that as it sets a small dip or holes appear in the top of the candle.

5 If this occurs, reheat the saved wax and pour into any holes or dips (if necessary you can use a cocktail stick to enlarge small holes to ensure they are completely filled with new wax). Do not pour over the original height of the wax.

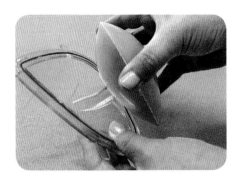

6 Leave the candle to set until completely cold. Remove the mould seal and the wick sustainer and the candle should easily come away from the mould. Leave to set and cure for 48 hours before burning.

USING LATEX RUBBER OR SILICONE MOULDS

1 Take a primed wick and thread it through the end of a wicking needle. Pierce the bottom of the latex rubber or silicone mould, making sure that the hole is exactly in the centre, and pull the wick through the hole in the mould.

2 Place the mould in a special holder, which are available for rubber moulds.

3 Alternatively, make a collar out of cardboard in which to insert the mould and suspend this over the rim of a glass or jug to hold it steady.

4 Now follow the instructions for pillar candles. Do not forget to treat the mould with a releasing agent if using beeswax. Once the candle is set, gently peel back the mould to reveal the candle. Leave to set and cure for 48 hours before burning.

5 If you are making candles with fruit-shaped moulds you may like to paint the wicks with brown coloured wax to make them look like the stems of the fruit.

CARDBOARD TUBES

Potato chip/crisp tubes are perfect for making pillar candles. Make sure that the bottom of the container is not completely flat and has a small lip so that you can seal your wick and the candle will still stand flat on the table.

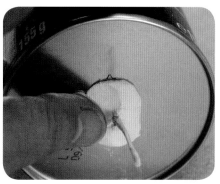

1 Thoroughly clean the inside of the mould, then pierce a hole centrally in the base using a metal skewer.

2 Thread the primed wick through the hole and seal with mould sealer or adhesive putty.

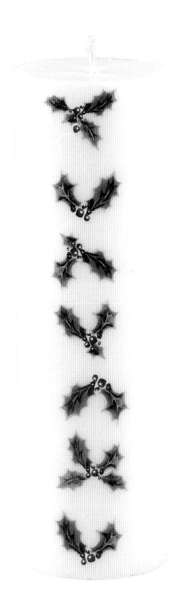

3 Secure the wick at the other end of the candle. To do this you can either use a wick sustainer or you can make a hole in the plastic lid of the container, cut the sides of the lid so that you can pour in the wax and thread the wick through the hole.

4 Now follow the instructions for making pillar candles. Leave to set and unmould the candle. It's often easiest to simply peel away the cardboard of the container. Leave to set for 48 hours before burning.

CONTAINER CANDLES

To make container candles, both your room and the containers should be at approximately 70°F (21°C); you can gently heat the containers in the oven or heat them with a hairdryer if they are really cold. The temperature difference between the wax and the container should be as little as possible so that the wax adheres well to the sides. If the temperature difference is too great, you may experience 'wet spots' or frosting on the sides of glass containers where small sections of the wax have pulled away from the edge. This creates no problem in the quality of your candle; it is just less aesthetically pleasing.

1 Take a pre-tabbed, waxed/primed wick and dab a piece of wax glue, a glue dot, or hot glue from a gun onto the base of the metal tab and affix to the bottom of the container.

2 Make sure that you place the wick exactly in the centre of the container otherwise the candle will burn unevenly.

3 If the container is a little deep for your hand to fully reach in to secure the wick tab, use a chopstick or end of a wooden spoon to press it in place.

4 Make sure that you wick the candle appropriately for your type of container. Refer to Selecting a Wick, pages 8–10.

5 Heat the wax to 155°F (68°C) or 190°F (87°C) if using powder dye. Colour and scent the wax and pour at between 125°F (51°C) and 155°F (68°C); see page 12. Leave to set and cure for 48 hours before burning.

MULTI-WICKED CONTAINER CANDLES

For container candles or pillar candles that are larger than 4in (10cm) in diameter, you will need to use more than one wick (see the wick guide on page 9). For a multi-wicked candle, lay chopsticks or wooden skewers across the top of the mould to help keep the wicks in position.

WOODEN WICKS

Wooden wicks are wicked in the same way as any other wick. They usually come with tabs (small metal discs) that you can glue to the bottom of your container as you would for a normal tabbed wick, although the wick can also be suspended.

1 Suspend the wick over the container and hold it in the correct position with wick sustainers. You could also use two wooden sticks held together with elastic bands.

2 When the candle is set, trim the wooden wick to approximately ¼in (0.5cm) with a pair of wood wick trimmers, (these are inexpensive and sold by candlemaking suppliers).

WHIPPED WAX

To make whipped wax for pillar candles, first make a base candle for decorating. Whipped wax has the texture and appearance of whipped cream or frosty snow and is particularly suited to food and snowy themes (make sure that food-type candles are labelled 'do not eat' and keep them well away from children).

1 Melt some pillar wax and leave it to cool. When it starts to pale up, whip it with a fork as if you are whipping cream.

2 As soon as the wax resembles whipped cream and is solid enough to hold its form, quickly apply it to the base candle.

3 If you work too slowly the wax will solidify and become crumbly. If this happens, simply reheat and start again.

DECORATING WHIPPED WAX

Decorative items such as embeds made from pillar wax or items made from beeswax sheets, such as rolled 'cherries' or 'flakes', can be gently pressed into the whipped wax while it is soft – but you will need to be fast as it will set quickly.

1 Tear off a small portion of the beeswax sheet.

2 Roll the wax into a ball between your forefinger and thumb.

3 Push the 'cherry' decoration into the whipped wax.

FLOATING CANDLES

As long as a candle is wider than it is tall it should float in water. Floating candles should be made from soya pillar blend wax or beeswax. Special floating candle moulds can be purchased or you can use miniature muffin trays or cookie cutter shapes.

1 Make up batches of scented wax in two or three colours, then pour into the moulds. Use a spoon to scoop up one colour and dribble it into the mould containing another colour to achieve a multicoloured effect.

2 Wait for the wax to set slightly and then pop in a pre-tabbed waxed wick. Make sure that the wick is primed so that it does not absorb water. If your candles are small you can use votive or tea light wicks.

DECORATING CANDLES

You can, of course, leave your candles plain and simple, but it can be fun to decorate them for an extra special effect. Over the next few pages, we show you ways of decorating and enhancing candles with cut-out wax shapes and transfers, by giving them a shimmering effect with overdips and pearlizers or by stencilling a pattern.

APPLIQUÉ

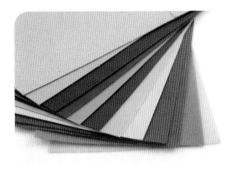

1 Appliqué wax sheets are available in a multitude of colours and metallics from which you can cut your own decorative shapes using sugarcraft cutters, and then affix to your candle. You can also buy ready-cut appliqué wax shapes.

2 To cut out a shape, gently press a cutter into the wax as if you were cutting a cookie. Alternatively, use a knife to cut freehand shapes. Warm the cut shape in your hands and press directly onto the candle. Alternatively, use a dab of wax glue to fix the shape to your candle.

CANDLE TRANSFERS

Some candle suppliers sell picture transfers, or metallic transfer sheets to apply to candles. These can be tricky to work with, but are effective. Place the transfer on the candle and rub the back to transfer the design. The transfer should adhere to the candle, but you may have to gently peel it off with your fingers. Try a sample first to make sure that it will transfer to your type or blend of wax before buying a lot of transfers.

BEESWAX SHEETS

Coloured sheets of honeycomb beeswax are available in lots of colours and can be used in a similar way to appliqué wax. Cut your desired shape and affix to your candle with wax glue. Pieces of beeswax sheet can also be rolled into tubes or moulded with the fingers to create shapes – make sure that the beeswax is at room temperature so that it is pliable.

OTHER IDEAS FOR DECORATING CANDLES

OVERDIPPING

Another way of giving your candle a colourful or shimmering finish is to overdip it. Cut the wick a little longer than normal, melt the wax and add either a contrasting colour or some metallic overdipping paste. Holding the candle by the wick, either half dip into the contrasting colour (for a two-tone effect) or dip the whole candle to entirely coat it with colour.

CANDLE GLITTER

Add a little sparkle to your candle with some candle glitter. There are various types available to buy, so follow your supplier's instructions.

CANDLE-DECORATING PENS

These candle pens come in a vast range of colours and metallics. They can be used to write or draw a unique design directly onto the candle.

STENCILLING OR STAMPING

Liven up a plain candle by stencilling or stamping a design onto it. Stamps and stencils can be purchased from craft shops or you can make your own stencil cut from paper. Pieces of old lace or paper doilies can create pretty patterns on wedding candles, particularly when used with metallic paints.

Fix the stencil to the candle and lightly spray a non-toxic paint over it. If using a sponge, dip it in a little acrylic paint and press over the stencil. Alternatively, paint a stamp with acrylic paint (practice on paper first) and roll from side to side on the candle. Ensure that you do not spray the paint near a naked flame or burning candle.

You can also stick non-flammable items such as metallic foil, gems, beads and shells to the outside of your candle. Fix them on by painting some melted wax glue to the back of the object.

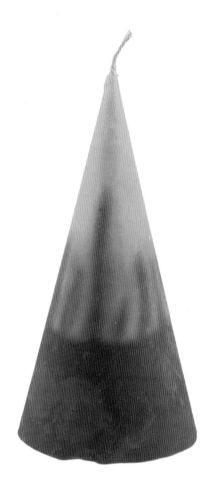

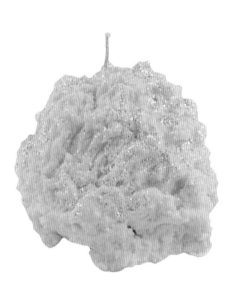

A candle decorated with glitter.

A tube of candle glitter.

Candle-decorating pens.

Test burning and safety

TEST BURNING A CANDLE

Don't forget to label your candles if test burning in a batch.

If you plan to sell batches of candles or give them away as presents, you must always test burn some samples first to calculate the burn rate, the suitability of the wick (see below), and to check the quality of the burn.

Test burning will enable you to check the 'hot scent throw' (how strong the fragrance is when the candle is lit), the 'cold scent throw' (how strong the fragrance is when the candle is unlit), the burn pool size, the flame size and the presence of sooting or other unwanted characteristics.

If you are testing a lot of candles, it's a good idea to label each one with a batch number and to record this on a test-burning sheet for future reference.

TEST DIFFERENT WICKS

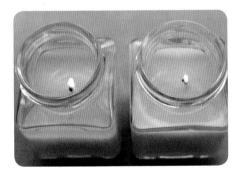

Test burning is the best way find the wick most suited to your candle.

Leave the candle to set or 'cure' for at least 48 hours. To save having to make a lot of samples of the same candle to test several different wicks, make a candle without a wick. Take a wicking needle, skewer or drill bit about the same diameter as the wick and pierce a hole in the candle where the wick should be. Insert a primed wick in the hole, light the candle and make a note of the burn qualities.

If you need to try a different-sized wick, take out the old wick while the wax is still melted, leave to set again, make another hole and insert a new wick.

However, if you wish to compare, for example, three candles with different wicks all burning alongside each other, it would be better to make three separate candles with three wicks.

HOW TO TEST BURN A CONTAINER CANDLE

1 Trim the wick to ¼in (0.5cm).

2 Measure the diameter of the candle in inches, i.e. 2in.

3 Burn the candle for the same number of hours, i.e. 2 hours.

4 In this length of time, you should achieve a burn pool depth (depth of melted wax) of ¼ to ½in (0.5 to 1cm).

5 The wax should be completely melted.

6 If you have a larger burn pool, the candle smokes, or the wick mushrooms badly (has an excessive build up of carbon), you may need to use a smaller wick, a different fragrance or less fragrance.

7 If you do not achieve the full ¼in (0.5cm) burn pool in the timescale calculated, try a larger wick.

CALCULATING THE BURN TIME OF A CANDLE

1 Weigh the candle (if using a container, subtract weight of the empty container from the total weight so you get only the weight of the wax ('start weight')	e.g. 7oz (200g)
2 Burn the candle for 3 hours ('test-burn' hours)	
3 Weigh the candle again ('end weight')	e.g. 6.3oz(180g)
4 Subtract the end weight from the start weight	e.g. 7oz (200g) − 6.3oz (180g) = 0.7oz (20g)
5 Divide the lost wax weight between the number of test-burn hours	e.g. 0.7oz (20g) ÷ 3 (hours) = 0.23oz (6.66g)
Summary Original candle weight Minus the weight after 3 test-burn hours = Lost wax during burning Divide by number of test-burn hours **This is the burn rate per hour**	7oz (200g) 6.3oz (180g) 0.7oz (20g) ÷ 3 (hours) = 0.23oz (6.66g)
Original candle weight Divide by hourly burn rate **This is the total burn rate**	7oz (200g) ÷ 0.23oz (6.66g) = 30 hours

The candle will therefore burn 0.23oz (6.66g) of wax per hour. If your original candle weight was 7oz (200g), this means that your candle will burn for approxiamately 30 hours.

IN THE EVENT OF A FIRE:

- Leave the melting pan where it is – do not pick it up or move it.

- Turn off the electric power or heat source.

- **DO NOT USE WATER** – wax is like oil, so never use water to extinguish a wax fire; instead smother the flames.

- Smother the flames with bicarbonate of soda, a fire blanket, fire extinguisher, damp cloth, metal lid or metal baking tray.

- Call the fire brigade.

FIRE PRECAUTIONS

Keep a tub of bicarbonate of soda (baking soda) next to your melting pot as it is good for smothering flames. It will not always be apparent when the wax is in danger of combusting, so you must check the temperature frequently.

Cleaning up spilt wax

If you spill soya wax on the floor or kitchen surface, leave it to set and simply scrape it up. Clean any excess with hot soapy water. If you spill soya wax on your clothing or carpet, wash it with hot soapy water.

If you spill beeswax on a carpet or clothing, lay some absorbent paper towels on top of the spillage and place a warm iron on top of the paper. This will melt the wax and the paper will absorb some of the melted wax. You will need to repeat this process, replacing the absorbent paper as the wax gets absorbed. Alternatively, you could place smaller items in the freezer, to let the intense cold solidify the wax, allowing it to be crumbled, or rub with an ice cube. If all else fails take your item of clothing to the dry cleaners.

IF YOU BURN YOUR SKIN WITH HOT WAX:

- Immediately immerse the burn in cool water.

- For mild burns treat with aloe vera or visit your pharmacy for over-the-counter burn treatments.

- If the burn blisters badly, turn off the source of heat melting the wax and go immediately to the nearest clinic or hospital.

LABELLING YOUR CANDLES

If you want to give your candles as a present or sell to the public, you **must** label them with fire safety precautions. Some, or all of the information below should be added to the candle label, depending on the type of candle.

Picture warnings can also be included. You may also be required to state burn times or the weight of the candle so contact your local or national trading standards department or candle guild for full advice on selling candles.

SAFETY WARNINGS:

• Never leave a burning candle unattended.

• Burn away from combustibles.

• Keep candles away from children and pets.

• Always burn candles away from draughts.

• Trim the wick to ¼in (0.5cm) before each burn and remove traces of carbon or match debris from the candle.

• On the first lighting of a candle, burn to a full burn pool to achieve even burning thereafter and to avoid a tunnelling effect on subsequent burns.

• Do not burn a candle for more than four hours at a time.

• Do not burn the last ½in (1cm) of container candles to avoid excess heating of the container.

• Place the candle on a heat-resistant surface.

• Tea lights should always be placed in an appropriate tea light holder and should never placed directly on to a surface.

Troubleshooting

Here are some of the common problems and solutions that may occur when you are making candles:

Problem	Solutions
The flame is large and smoking	Trim the wick to ¼in (0.5cm) or use a smaller wick.
Mushrooming: carbon or soot build-up on wick	Wick is too large; try a different size or type of wick. Fragrance or essential oil is incompatible or you have used too much fragrance or essential oil.
The flame is small and the wick is drowning or extinguished in wax	The wick is too small and cannot consume all of the melted wax. Change to a larger wick.
Wax is sweating on top of a soya candle	Too much fragrance or essential oil, or the fragrance is incompatible with the wax. Change or cut down on either or both.
Glass container candle appears to have wet spots or areas of different-coloured soya wax on the sides of the container	The difference between the temperature of the containers and the wax may have been too great and the wax has pulled away from the container in parts and not adhered to the sides. Heat the containers in an oven or with a hairdryer if they are too cold – they should be room temperature. The candles have cooled too quickly. The room temperature should be around 70°F (21°C). Candles have been stored at too low a temperature, they should be stored at around 70°F (21°C).
A chalky white substance has appeared on the top of a soya candle	This is known as 'frosting' or 'bloom' and is a change in the crystal structure of the wax similar to the bloom that can appear on chocolates. This can result if: • The pouring temperature was too high • The candles were cooled too quickly • Storage of candles was too cold (this will disappear in a few days if the candles are moved to a storage area of 70°F/21°C) • The containers were too close together while cooling. They need to be at least ½in (1cm) apart so that the air can circulate. The containers should remain open for 24 hours while setting Heat the surface with a hairdryer or heat gun to remove frosting.
Holes or craters have appeared in the top of a soya container candle	Try pouring the wax at a lower temperature. Reduce the temperature in 10°F (or 6°C) increments and record your findings. It may also be due to trapped air. Make sure you pour the wax slowly to reduce air bubbles. Heat the surface with a hairdryer or heat gun to even out any holes; this will briefly melt the wax and smooth the surface again. When the trapped air rises to the surface, pop it with a pin.
Candle burns a tunnel of wax downwards in my container	The wick is too small. You didn't burn the candle for long enough on the first burn to achieve a full burn pool – this changes the structure of the wax so that each burn pool thereafter continues to produce a full burn pool.

Green tea

Rummage around charity shops and flea markets to find pretty tea cups, tea pots or egg cups to use as unique and attractive containers. Light them at a garden tea party on a lovely summer day.

INGREDIENTS

- 28oz (700ml or 805g) soya container wax
- See the wick guide on page 9 to select a wick for testing
- Meadow green colour
- 2 tablespoons (30ml) green tea candle fragrance oil

CONTAINERS
China tea cups

QUANTITY
This recipe will make approx. 4 candles

See pages 18–19 for instructions on making container candles

Kitchen candle

Food smells delicious when it is being prepared and cooked but once the meal is over, the smells are not so attractive. Burn one of these herbal candles to help remove those unpleasant aromas and make your kitchen fresh again.

INGREDIENTS

- 10oz (250ml or 290g) soya container wax
- See the wick guide on page 9 to select a wick for testing
- 1 teaspoon (5ml) lemongrass essential oil
- ¼ teaspoon (1.25ml) basil essential oil
- ¼ teaspoon (1.25ml) lime essential oil

CONTAINERS

Empty spice jars

QUANTITY

This recipe will make 2 candles

See pages 18–19 for instructions on making container candles

Sundae best

You will probably not want to burn this mouth-watering candle as it looks just like the real thing, so place it on a kitchen shelf or sideboard and have a calorie-free peek every now and then if you are watching your weight.

INGREDIENTS

- 12oz (300ml or 345g) soya container wax
- 4oz (100ml or 115g) soya pillar blend wax
- ¼ sheet brown beeswax, small piece of red beeswax sheet
- See the wick guide on page 9 to select a wick for testing
- Pink and red (bottom layer), light pink (middle layer) colours
- 1 tablespoon (15ml) strawberry fragrance oil (container),
- 1 teaspoon (5ml) vanilla candle fragrance oil (topping)

CONTAINERS

Glass sundae dish

QUANTITY

This recipe will make 1 candle

ADDITIONAL INSTRUCTIONS

Roll the red beeswax into a ball and brown into cigar shape. Wick candle, pour the first layer, leave to set slightly then pour next layer. Leave to set until firm. Make whipped pillar wax and place on top. Press cherry and chocolate flake into the soft wax.

See page 55 for instructions on using beeswax sheets and page 54 for using whipped wax

Boudoir chic

Turn your bedroom into a 1930s glamour pad. Look for retro glass trinket sets in flea markets or on auction sites and fill with feminine, floral-scented wax. Then light a candle and pad around in your fluffy-heeled slippers.

INGREDIENTS

- 6oz (150ml or 170g) container soya wax
- See the wick guide on page 9 to select a wick for testing
- 1 teaspoon (5ml) rose candle fragrance oil
- 1 teaspoon (5ml) non-discolouring vanilla candle fragrance oil
- Light pink colour

CONTAINERS

Pretty glass dishes

QUANTITY

This recipe will make approx. 3 small candles

See pages 18–19 for instructions on making container candles

Pillar of strength

Traditionally used in many religious ceremonies, pillar candles give us the impression of purity and strength. These pillars of ivory can be simply decorated with green foliage or with a riot of colour for a festival or wedding.

INGREDIENTS
- 36.5oz (900ml or 1.035kg) soya pillar blend wax
- See the wick guide on page 9 to select a wick for testing
- 3 tablespoons (45ml) holly candle fragrance oil
- Holly leaf transfers for decoration (optional)

MOULD
Clean empty potato chip or crisp tube

QUANTITY
This recipe will make 1 candle

ADDITIONAL INSTRUCTIONS
Make sure that your candle is more than 2½in (6cm) in diameter when using soya pillar blend wax. Rub holly leaf transfers onto the candle if desired.

See page 15 for instructions on making pillar candles, page 17 for instructions on using cardboard tubes and page 21 for how to apply candle transfers

Spruce up

There is nothing like a walk in an ancient forest to give you a strengthening, grounded feeling. Pine is said to engergize your senses, clear your mind, nose and sinuses and help relieve breathing conditions.

INGREDIENTS
- 8oz (200ml or 230g) white beeswax
- See the wick guide on page 9 to select a wick for testing or use a square-braided wick to match your candle's diameter
- 1 teaspoon (5ml) pine essential oil
- 1 teaspoon (5ml) cedarwood essential oil
- Cocoa brown colour

MOULD
Homemade mould using liquid latex rubber

QUANTITY
This recipe will make 1 candle

ADDITIONAL INSTRUCTIONS
If using soya pillar blend wax instead of beeswax, make sure that your candle is more than 2½in (6cm) in diameter.

See page 7 for instructions on making rubber moulds and page 16 for how to use them

Old flame

Flare up that passion within and rekindle an old romance or put some fire back into your relationship. This recipe is made with sensual essential oils that are known for their aphrodisiac properties.

INGREDIENTS
- 6oz (150ml or 170g) white beeswax
- See the wick guide on page 9 to select a wick for testing (use the diameter from middle of candle to work out wick size)
- 1 teaspoon (5ml) rose geranium essential oil
- ¼ teaspoon (1.25ml) patchouli essential oil
- ⅛ teaspoon (0.6ml) ginger essential oil
- ⅛ teaspoon (0.6ml) ylang ylang essential oil
- Orange and red colours

MOULD
Cone or triangular-shaped plastic mould

QUANTITY
This recipe will make 1 candle

ADDITIONAL INSTRUCTIONS
Wick the candle. Melt wax, add orange colour and then pour. Leave until a skin has set. Add the red colour and pour over the orange. Using a wicking needle, poke through to orange layer so some red leaks in. Pour on the rest and leave to set.

See page 15 for instructions on making pillar candles

Lemon-aid

A bowl of zesty citrus fruits makes a fresh display and uplifting scent in the kitchen. Use pre-made rubber fruit moulds or make your own using rubber latex and real fruit.

INGREDIENTS
- 7oz (175ml or 200g) white beeswax
- See the wick guide on page 9 to select a wick for testing or use a square-braided wick to match your candle's diameter
- 1 teaspoon (5ml) lemon or lime or sweet orange essential oils
- Yellow, green or orange and a small amount of brown colour

MOULD
Pre-made or homemade rubber fruit mould

QUANTITY
The recipe will make 1 candle

ADDITIONAL INSTRUCTIONS
Unless you have made lots of moulds, which are very time consuming, you will have to make one fruit at a time. Spray the inside of the rubber mould with silicone spray to make unmoulding easier. For the stalks, melt a small amount of wax and colour brown. Either dip the candle wick into the brown wax to make the stalks lifelike or use a paintbrush to paint the coloured wax onto the wicks.

See page 7 for instructions on making rubber moulds

Float away

Float these pretty multicoloured candles in a glass bowl with other summer flower heads. They make an attractive addition to a summer party, wedding or celebration table. Breathe in the delicate scent and let your mind float away.

INGREDIENTS
- 6oz (150ml or 170g) soya pillar blend wax
- See the wick guide on page 9 to select a wick for testing
- 1½ teaspoon (7.5ml) buttercup (or other floral) candle fragrance oil
- Various, mixed colours

MOULDS
Flower floating candle moulds

QUANTITY
This recipe will make approx. 6 candles

ADDITIONAL INSTRUCTIONS
With a spoon, scoop up a little wax of each colour and dribble into the next mould to achieve a multicoloured effect.

See page 20 for instructions on making floating candles

Completely potty

Put your old garden pots to good use and help keep those bugs at bay. Insects do not like citrus scents and lighting one of these outdoor candles near your picnic table may make them think twice before dining with you.

INGREDIENTS
- 22oz (550ml or 630g) soya container wax
- See the wick guide on page 9 to select a wick for testing (or use two smaller wicks if using a container larger than 4in/10cm)
- 1 tablespoon (15ml) lemongrass essential oil
- 2 teaspoons (10ml) citronella essential oil
- Green colour

CONTAINER
Extra large garden pot. For a smaller, less expensive candle use a smaller plant pot, garden urn, or preserve jar

QUANTITY
This recipe will make 1 large candle

ADDITIONAL INSTRUCTIONS
If your container has a hole in the bottom, fix a pebble over the hole with hot glue, glue dot or wax glue.

See pages 18-19 for instructions on making container candles